ABOUT THE AUTHOR

NORMAN MAILER was born in 1923 and published his first book, *The Naked and the Dead*, in 1948. *The Armies of the Night* won the National Book Award and the Pulitzer Prize in 1969; Mailer received another Pulitzer in 1980 for *The Executioner's Song*. He lives in Provincetown, Massachusetts, and Brooklyn, New York. His most recent work is *The Spooky Art: Some Thoughts on Writing*.

WHY ARE WE AT WAR?

Norman Mailer

WHY ARE WE AT WAR?

RANDOM HOUSE TRADE PAPERBACKS

NEW YORK

TO NORRIS

CONTENTS

Part I

IX/XI

PREFACE

As you will see by turning the page, this book begins with an account by my old friend Dotson Rader of his experiences during the morning and afternoon of 9/11.

One year later, we got together to do an interview for the London *Sunday Times Magazine* about the reverberations of that event upon American life. I remember the stimulation, the kick-start if you will, that was provided by Dotson's eloquence on the subject. Before it was over, I talked a great deal that day, and much of it is reprinted here, as well as a number of remarks I have added to what was said then and have been thinking about since.

9/11 is one of those events that will never fade out of our history, for it was not only a cataclysmic disaster but a symbol, gargantuan and mysterious, of we know not what, an obsession that will return through decades to come.

Indeed, this book, which looks to give some fresh notion of why America is in a state of war with Iraq, would have no existence without the fall of the Twin Towers, and so it seemed appropriate to begin with Dotson Rader's description of what must have been the most surrealistic morning in the archives of New York's history.

1

DOTSON RADER: I was at home in my apartment on East Eighty-fifth Street in Manhattan when the first of the Twin Towers was hit by one of the planes. But at the time I didn't know it had happened. Later that morning I tried to make a phone call, and my phone was dead. So I got dressed and went outside. I live four blocks from Gracie Mansion, the official residence of the mayor. None of the pay phones on the street worked. People were wandering oddly about, sort

of dazed, as if kind of lost. It was very strange. I
started walking downtown—it was a bright, almost hot day in New York. I was supposed to
have lunch with a friend on Fifty-seventh Street,
and I was walking down Third Avenue to meet
him at the restaurant. When I reached Sixty-
fourth Street, I noticed this huge, bubbling cloud
in the sky above Manhattan south of me. The rest
of the sky was blue and clear. I didn't know what
it was. And then, looking down Third Avenue, six
or seven blocks away, as far as I could see, I suddenly noticed a vast throng of people, a flood of
humanity, like a slow wave rolling north up the avenue. Many of them were men in white shirts. They
were the office workers from Wall Street, fleeing
the disaster. This quiet mass of people, tens of
thousands, was walking up the island like a funeral
procession and turning at Fifty-seventh Street and
then moving as one toward the 59th Street Bridge
to cross over out of the island. And I thought,
"Jesus! Is this Christ's Second Coming?" Because
they were in white, covered in dust, and they

looked stunned, and they were speaking in whispers, like kids in church. I thought it was the Rapture and Jesus was calling his saints home, and that I was being left behind. That was my initial feeling.

NORMAN MAILER: Wouldn't that be it? Jesus had come and everybody has gone to meet him by crossing the bridge from Manhattan to Queens. That does capture my pessimism concerning cosmic matters. [*laughter*]

DOTSON RADER: Okay. Where were you on September 11? How did you learn about the terrorist attacks, and what was your initial reaction?

NORMAN MAILER: I was in my house up here in Provincetown. I remember a phone call telling me to turn on the TV. While I was watching I called my youngest daughter, Maggie. I have an apartment in Brooklyn Heights, and she was staying there with a friend. You can see lower Manhattan and the Twin Towers from that apartment. Our windows look across the East River. So Maggie had witnessed the first attack and was terribly affected by it. Then, while we were on the phone, the second plane hit the other building. I'm still watching on TV. In Brooklyn, Maggie and her friend are both seeing it through the window as well as viewing it on TV. That was a considerable shock. Why? Because the one thing TV always promises us is that, deep down, what we see on television is not real. It's why there's always that subtle numbness to TV. The most astonishing events, even terrifying events, nonetheless have a touch of nonexistence when seen on the tube. They don't terrify us. We see something that's hideous, but we're not shocked proportionally. It's why we can watch anything on TV.

Now, there are exceptions. The shooting of Lee Harvey Oswald by Jack Ruby was one; the second plane striking the second Tower; the collapse of the Towers. TV at that moment was no longer a coat of insulation between us and the horrific. When broken, the impact is enormous.

DOTSON RADER: What struck me, what I'll never forget, is the silence. Everyone was just silent. Or if they spoke, they whispered. It was like everyone was at a funeral. And this went on for hours and hours. Occasionally, the silence was broken by an ambulance or police siren. And what I'd never seen in New York before—military jets started flying over the island, because they started closing Manhattan down. The military started showing up in the streets. I thought, What in God's name is happening?

2

What in God's name was happening? It is one thing to hear a mighty explosion. It is another to recognize some time after the event that one has been deafened by it. The United States was going through an identity crisis. Questions about our nature as a country were being asked that most good American men and women had never posed to themselves before. Questions such as, Why are we so hated? How could anyone resent us that much? We do no evil. We believe in goodness and freedom. Who are we, then?

Are we not who we think we are? More pressing, who are "they?" What does it all mean?

Simple questions. Blank as white and empty pages. We were going through an identity crisis, and that is an incomparable experience. The ego has been disrupted. It has been pre-empted. Most of us look to command an ego that will keep us reasonably efficient while we carry out our personal projects. We see ourselves as husbands or wives, as brave or prudent, reliable or decent, or certain egos may depend on the right to excuse themselves—as flighty, or in search of friendship, which, once found, will take care of all else.

In that sense, it hardly matters what kind of firm notion the ego attaches to itself. That, from the need of the ego, is less important than the ongoing expectation that the notion will rest reasonably stable. Upon that depends our identity, that firm seat which offers the psyche an everyday working notion of who we are (good-looking or good-looking enough—whatever serves).

An identity crisis builds slowly, or it can strike

like a thunderclap, but the effect is unmistakable. One can no longer offer a firm declaration of who one is. The seat upon which the ego depends has been slipped out from under. The psyche is in a sprawl. The simplest questions become difficult to answer.

A mass identity crisis for all of America descended upon us after 9/11, and our response was wholly comprehensible. We were plunged into a fever of patriotism. If our long-term comfortable and complacent sense that America was just the greatest country ever had been brought into doubt, the instinctive reflex was to reaffirm ourselves. We had to overcome the identity crisis—hell, overpower it, wave a flag.

We had had a faith. The ship of the United States was impregnable and had been on a great course. We were steering ourselves into a great future. All of a sudden, not to be able to feel like that was equal to seeing oneself as a traitor to the grand design. So we gathered around George W. Bush. That he had not been elected by a majority even became a species of new strength for him. The transient, still-forming, fresh national identity could not for a moment contemplate the fact that maybe Bush should not even be in the White House. Why? Because now the country had to be saved. A horror had come upon us. There were people on earth so eager to destroy us that they were ready to immolate themselves. That went right to the biblical root. Samson had pulled down the pillars of the Temple. Now there were all these Muslim Samsons. A ripple went through the country, a determining wind. In its wake, flags rippled everywhere. Nearly everyone in America was waving a flag.

For a few of us, this great indiscriminate wave of patriotism was not a joy to behold. "Patriotism," after all, "is the last refuge of a scoundrel." So said H. L. Mencken, or was it Samuel Johnson? One could argue over the source but not the sentiment.

3

DOTSON RADER: Are they even waving flags up in Provincetown?

NORMAN MAILER: They are. We had a parade in Provincetown on the Fourth of July, 2002. A rather nice looking, pleasant fellow—he looked to me like a young liberal lawyer—came up and smiled and handed me a small American flag. And I looked at him and just shook my head. And he walked on. It wasn't an episode in any way. He came over with a half-smile and walked away with a half-smile. But I was furious at myself afterward for not saying, "You don't have to wave a flag to be a patriot." By July 2002, it bothered me a good deal. Free-floating patriotism seemed like a direct measure of our free-floating anxiety.

Take the British for contrast. The British have a love of their country that is profound. They can revile it, tell dirty stories about it, give you dish on all the imperfects who are leading the country. But their patriotism is deep. In America it's as if we're playing musical chairs, and you shouldn't get caught without a flag or you're out of the game. Why do we need all this reaffirmation? It's as if we're a three-hundred-pound man who's seven feet tall, superbly shaped, absolutely powerful, and yet every three minutes he's got to reaffirm the fact that his armpits have a wonderful odor. We don't need compulsive, self-serving patriotism. It's odious. When you have a great country, it's your duty to be critical of it so it can become even greater. But culturally, emotionally, we are growing more arrogant, more vain. We're losing a sense of the beauty not only of democracy but also of its peril.

Democracy is built upon a notion that is exquisite and dangerous. It virtually states that if the will of the populace is freely expressed, more good than bad will result. When America began, it was the first time in the history of civilization that a nation dared to make an enormous bet founded on this daring notion—that there is more good than bad in people. Until then, the prevailing assumption had been that the powers at the top knew best; people were no good and had to be controlled. Now we have to keep reminding ourselves that just because we've been a great democracy, it doesn't guarantee we're going to continue to be one. Democracy is existential. It changes. It changes all the time. That's one reason why I detest promiscuous patriotism. You don't take democracy for granted. It is always in peril. We all know that any man or woman can go from being a relatively good person to a bad one. We can all become corrupted, or embittered. We can be swallowed by our miseries in life, become weary, give up. The fact that we've been a great democracy doesn't mean we will automatically keep being one if we keep waving the flag. It's ugly. You take a monarchy for granted, or a fascist state. You have to. That's the given. But a democracy changes all the time.

4

The fear that waved the flag in every hand was our nightmare of terrorism. Nightmares tell us that life is absurd, unreasonable, unjust, warped, crazy, and ridiculously dangerous. Terorrism suggests that your death will have no relation to your life, as if your death will also produce an identity crisis.

Implicit in our attitude toward our own end is that, for most of us, there is a logic within it. We spend much of our lives searching for that logic. We live in a certain manner. We act out some of our virtues and vices; we restrain others. From the sum of all those actions and abstentions will come our final disease. That is our assumption, at least for most of us. It can even be seen as a logical conclusion. We pay with our bodies for the sins and excesses of our minds and hearts. It is almost as if we want it that way. Our psyches are jarred, even tortured, by absurdity, and confirmed, sometimes soothed even, by a reasonable recognition of consequence.

Terrorism, however, shatters this equation. The comprehension of our death that we have worked to obtain is lost. Our ability to find meaning in our lives is lost.

5

DOTSON RADER: So, do you hate terrorism?

NORMAN MAILER: I hate it; I loathe it. Since I believe in reincarnation, I think the character of your death is tremendously important to you. One wants to be able to meet one's death with a certain seriousness. To me, it is horrible to be killed without warning. Because you can't prepare yourself in any last way for your next existence. So your death contributes to absurdity. Terrorism's ultimate tendency is to make life absurd.

When I consider the nearly three thousand people who died in the Twin Towers disaster, it's not the ones who were good fathers and good mothers and good daughters, good brothers and good husbands or sons, that I mourn most. It's the ones who came from families that were less happy. When a good family member dies, there's a tenderness and a sorrow that can restore life to those who are left behind. But when someone dies who's half loved and half hated by his own family, whose children, for example, are always trying to get closer to that man or to that woman and don't quite succeed, then the aftereffect is obsessive. Those are the ones who are hurt the most. I won't call them dysfunctional families, but it's into the less successful families that terrorism bites most deeply. Because there is that terrible woe that one can't speak to the dead parent or the dead son or daughter or dead mate; one can't set things right anymore. One was planning to, one was hoping to, and now it's lost forever. That makes it profoundly obsessive.

DOTSON RADER: Would you define terrorism as wickedness, as an evil?

NORMAN MAILER: To me there's a great difference between doing evil and being wicked. I don't use the words interchangeably. People who are wicked are always raising the ante without knowing quite what they're doing. Most of us are wicked to a good degree. Most of us who are game players or adventurous in any way are wicked. We raise the ante all the time without knowing what the results might be. We're mischievous, if you will.

Evil, however, is to have a pretty good idea of the irreparable damage you're going to do and then proceed to do it. In that sense, yes, terrorism is evil.

However, it's worth trying to understand terrorism in the context by which the terrorists see it. They feel they're gouging out an octopus that's looking to destroy their world. They feel virtuous. The individual terrorist might be violating every single rule in Islam—he might, for example, be a drug addict or booze a lot—but at the end, he still believes he will find redemption through immolation. He is one small shard in the spiritual wreckage of the world right now. After all, in America there are a great many people on the right who are going around saying, Let's kill all the Muslims; let's simplify the world. You think Islam has a special purchase on terrorism?

DOTSON RADER: What I think is that we are facing a war of civilizations between an Islamic cult of death—

NORMAN MAILER: Wait a minute. Cult of death? You're going too far. For every Muslim who believes in your cult of death, thousands don't. People who are ready to sacrifice their lives form a very special group. They don't need big numbers.

DOTSON RADER: But millions cheer them in the streets.

NORMAN MAILER: Oh, it's easy to cheer. I can cheer athletes who score winning touchdowns when I don't know the first thing about them. I'm cheering for an idea, my team! That's one thing. It's another to shed your own blood. There's a gulf between the two. Many a Muslim who hates us is nowhere near to being a terrorist.

Still, so many of them do hate us.

DOTSON RADER: Okay, recognizing that, why? Why are we so hated?

NORMAN MAILER: To some degree it's envy. Some human emotions are obvious. But we're also hated for more intrusive reasons. Corporate capitalism does have this tendency to take over large parts of the economies of other countries. Often we are the next thing to cultural barbarians. We don't always pay attention to what we are trampling. What intensifies the anger is how often we are successful in these commercial invasions. You go into a McDonald's in Moscow and there are marble floors. The Russian equivalent of young corporate executives are phoning each other across the room on their cell phones. They're proud of that. I spoke once at Moscow State University to a class that was studying American literature. One of the students asked me, "Is there anything in our economy that compares to American economy?" I said, "Yes. Your McDonald's are better than ours." And they loved it. They were delighted. They had something they could do that was better than us. It was as if Brooklyn College were playing the University of Nebraska in football. The score had been one hundred to nothing, but then they kicked a field goal—it's now one hundred to three. And the Brooklyn College stands went crazy. So, by the same token, those are the people—and these are the young people in Moscow—who are reacting positively to American corporate culture.

Now think of all the other people in Russia who hate the very thought that not only were they bankrupted by the United States, not only were they betrayed by a communism that many of them had believed in, but now on top of it they're being culturally invaded by these people with their money-grubbing notions of food. And, worse, the young love it. The young are leaving them. So the hatred toward America intensifies.

Now, take the West's cultural invasion into Islam. The Muslim reaction is that Islam is endangered by modern technology and corporate capitalism. They see everything in America as aiming to destroy the basis of Islam. The huge freedom given to women in American culture is seen as an outrage by orthodox Muslims. American TV they find licentious in the extreme. They feel all that Islam stands for is going to be eroded by American culture. So, to repeat: The core of the hatred of Muslims toward us is the fear that they're going to lose their own people to Western values. Maybe half the people in Muslim countries may want secretly to be free of Islam. And so the ones who retain the old religion become extreme in response. Many Muslims can put Christian fundamentalists to shame by the intensity of their belief. It's an interesting belief, after all.

There is one fascinating element in Islam, which is the idea that all Muslims are equal before God, a tremendous egalitarian concept. Like all organized religion, Islam ends up being the perversion of itself in practice. Just as in Christianity, compassion is supposed to be the greatest good, but its present exercise in the world seems to be a study in military power and greed. In Islam, no Muslim has the right to consider himself superior to another Muslim. What happens in reality is that you have oppressive societies run for the wealthy, with the poor getting less and less—tremendous economic inequalities in many a Muslim society. And tyrannical people in the seats of power.

Now, of course, the Koran, like the Old and New Testaments, has something in it for everyone. You can run north, run south, blow east, you can blow west. But there have been numerous revolutions within Islam over the centuries to restore its original beliefs. There is no understanding of Islam until one recognizes that Muslims who are truly devoted feel they are in a direct relationship with God. Their Islamic culture is the most meaningful experience of their lives, and their culture is being infiltrated. They feel the kind of outrage toward us that, let's say, a good Catholic would know if a black mass were performed in his church.

DOTSON RADER: But if that's true, if that's what the motivation is about, then there's no fixing it.

NORMAN MAILER: There's no quick fix. In fact, I'll go so far as to say that this is a war between those who believe the advance of technology is the best solution for human ills and those who believe that we got off the track somewhere a century ago, two centuries ago, five centuries ago, and we've been going in the wrong direction ever since, that the purpose of human beings on earth is not to obtain more and more technological power but to refine our souls. This is the deep divide that now goes on, even with many Americans. You know, what does it profit me if I gain the entire world and lose my soul?

Now, I don't want to paint myself into a corner where I am defending Islam. I'm sure they have as many sons of bitches as we have, maybe more. They probably have more in that they suffer lousier living conditions and they're under more tension. Muslims also bear a huge sense of shame, because they were a superior civilization around 1200, 1300 A.D., the most advanced culture then, and now they lag behind. There is a deep sense of failure among them. Think of those periods in your life when you felt you were a failure, and recall the bitterness, the anger, the disturbance. Multiply that by the followers of a faith, and that gives some sense of how bad it can get.

We in the West have this habit of looking for solutions. Part of the spirit of technology is to assume that there's always a solution to a problem, or something damn close to one. There may be no solution this time. This may be the beginning of an international cancer we cannot cure. What's in the mind of a cancer cell? Doubtless, its basic desire is to kill as many cells and invade as many organs as it can. So, too, the greater number of people the terrorists can wipe out, the happier they're going to be. Before you feel too righteous and outraged, however, let me ask: Did Harry Truman shiver in his bed at the thought that a hundred thousand people had been killed in Hiroshima and another hundred thousand in Nagasaki two days later, or was he proud that he had won the war?

6

And, one could add, won it by extraordinary means, never employed before. The explosion of the first atom bomb had an immensely greater effect upon human identity, worldwide human identity, than 9/11; yes, an order of magnitude more. We've never recovered from the knowledge that our earthly universe is chained to a bomb larger than human measure. So many of the roots of human history were pulled out by that bomb, and we have been paying the price ever since.

Part II

WHY ARE WE AT WAR?

ADDRESS TO THE COMMONWEALTH CLUB,
SAN FRANCISCO, FEBRUARY 20, 2003

It is probably true that at the beginning of the present push of the administration to go to war, the connections between Saddam Hussein and Osama bin Laden were minimal. Each, on the face of it, had to distrust the other. From Saddam's point of view, bin Laden was the most troublesome kind of man, a religious zealot, that is to say a loose cannon, a warrior who could not be controlled. To bin Laden, Saddam was an irreligious brute, an unbalanced fool whose boldest ventures invariably crashed.

The two were in competition as well. Each would look to control the future of the Muslim world, bin Laden conceivably for the greater glory of Allah and Saddam for the earthly delight of vastly augmenting his power. In the old days, in the nineteenth century, when the British had their empire, the Raj would have had the skill to set those two upon each other. It was the old rule of many a Victorian crazy house: Let the madmen duke it out, then jump the one or two who are left.

Today, however, these aims are different. Security is considered insecure unless the martial results are absolute. So the first American reaction to September 11 was to plan to destroy bin Laden and al Qaeda. When the campaign in Afghanistan failed, however, to capture the leading protagonist, even proved unable, indeed, to conclude whether he was alive or dead, the game had to shift. Our White House decided the real pea was under another shell. Not al Qaeda but Iraq.

Political leaders and statesmen are serious men even when they appear to be fools, and it is rare to find them acting without some deeper reason they can offer to themselves. It is these covert motives in the Bush administration upon which I would like to speculate here. I will attempt to understand what the President and his inner cohort see as the logic of their present venture.

———

Let me begin with Colin Powell's presentation before the U.N. on February 5, 2003. Up to a point, it was well detailed and ready to prove (to no one's dramatic surprise) that Saddam Hussein was violating every rule of the inspectors that he could get away with. Saddam, after all, had a keen nose for the vagaries of history. He understood that the longer one could delay powerful statesmen, the more they might weary of the soul-deadening boredom of dealing with a consummate liar who was artfully free of all the bonds of obligation and cooperation. It is no small gift to be an absolute liar. If you never tell the truth, you are virtually as safe as an honest man who never utters an untruth. When informed that you just swore to the opposite today of what you avowed yesterday, you remark, "I never said that," or should the words be on record, you declare that you are grossly misinterpreted. Rich confusion is sown, teeming with permutations.

So, Saddam had managed to survive seven years of inspection from 1991 to 1998. He had made deals—most of them under the counter—with the French, the Germans, the Russians, the Jordanians; the list is long. He also knew how to play on the sympathies of the third world. He convinced many a good heart. The continuing cruelty of America was starving the Iraqi children. The Iraqi children were, in large part, seriously malnourished by the embargo Saddam had brought upon himself, but indeed, if they had been healthy, he would have kept a score of six-year-olds starving long enough to dispatch a proper photograph around the globe. He was no good and he could prove it. He did so well at the games he played that he succeeded in declaring the inspections at an end by 1998.

There had been talk before, and there was certainly talk then in the White House, that we had to send troops into Iraq as our reply to such flouting of the agreement. Unfortunately, Clinton's adventure with Monica Lewinsky had left him a paralyzed warrior. In the midst of his public scandal, he could not afford to shed one drop of American blood. The proof was in Kosovo, where no American infantry went in with NATO and our bombers never dropped their product from any height within range of Serbian anti-aircraft. We did it all from fifteen thousand feet up. So Iraq was out of the question. Al Gore was a hawk at the time, ready, doubtless, to improve his future campaign image and rise thereby from wonk to stud—a necessary qualification for the presidency—but Clinton's vulnerability stifled all that.

So in 1998, Saddam Hussein got away with it. There had been no inspections since. Colin Powell's speech was full of righteous indignation at the barefaced and heinous bravado of Saddam the Evil, but Powell was, of course, too intelligent a man to be surprised by these discoveries of malfeasance. The speech was an attempt to heat up America's readi-

ness to go to war. By the measure of our polls, half
of the citizenry were unready. And this part of his
speech certainly succeeded. The proof was that a
good many Democratic senators who had been on
the fence declared that they were in on the venture
now; yes, they too were ready for war, God bless us.

The major weakness in Powell's presentation of the
evidence was, however, the evidential link of Iraq to
al Qaeda. It was, given the powerful auspices of the
occasion, more than a bit on the sparse side. With the
exception of Britain, the states with veto power in
the Security Council, the French, the Chinese, and
the Russians, were obviously not eager to satisfy the
Bush passion to go to war as soon as possible. They
wanted time to intensify inspections. They looked to
containment as a solution.

Not a week later, al Jazeera offered a recorded
broadcast by bin Laden which gave a few hints that
he and Saddam were now ready, conceivably, to
enter into direct contact, even though he called the

"socialists" in Baghdad "infidels." But this last statement was in immediate contradiction to what he
had just finished saying a moment earlier: "It does
no hurt under these conditions [of attack by the
West] that the interests of Muslims [will ultimately]
contradict the interest of the socialists in the fight
against the Crusaders."

Bin Laden may have chosen to be ambiguous and
two-sided in his remarks, but the suggestion of
a common interest, despite all, between al Qaeda
and Saddam was also there. Was it finally happening?
Had the enemy of Saddam's enemy now become
Saddam's friend? If so, that could prove a disaster.
We might vanquish Iraq and still suffer from the ca-
tastrophe we claimed to be going to war to avert.
Iraq's weapons of mass destruction could yet belong
to bin Laden.

Without those weapons, al Qaeda would have to
scrape and scratch. But if Saddam were to make
transfer of even a sizable fraction of his biowarfare
and chemical stores, bin Laden would be consider-
ably more dangerous. The inner diktat of George W.

Bush to go to war with Iraq as rapidly as possible now had to face the possibility that Saddam had come up with an exceptional countermove. Was he saying, in effect, "Allow me to string along the inspections, and you are still relatively safe. You may be certain I will not rush to give my very best stuff to Osama bin Laden so long as we can keep playing this inspection game back and forth, back and forth. Go to war with me, however, and Osama will smile. I may go down in flames, but he and his people will be happy. Be certain, he wants you to go to war with me."

Since the sequence of these kinds of moves was present from the beginning, it could be asked, as indeed more than a few Americans were now asking: How did we allow such choices in the first place— these hellish Hobson's choices?

Meanwhile, the world was reacting in horror to the Bush agenda for war. The European edition of *Time* magazine had been conducting a poll on its website: "Which country poses a greater danger to world peace in 2003?" With 318,000 votes cast, the responses were: North Korea, 7 percent; Iraq, 8 percent; the United States, 84 percent . . .

As John le Carré had put it to *The Times* of London: "America has entered one of its periods of historic madness, but this is the worst I can remember."

Harold Pinter no longer chose to be subtle in language:

> . . . The American administration is now a bloodthirsty wild animal. Bombs are its only vocabulary. Many Americans, we know, are horrified by the posture of their government, but seem to be helpless.
>
> Unless Europe finds the solidarity, intelligence, courage and will to challenge and resist American power, Europe itself will deserve Alexander Herzen's declaration "We are not the doctors. We are the disease."

According to Reuters, on February 15, more than 4 million people "from Bangkok to Brussels, from Canberra to Calcutta ... took to the streets to pillory Bush as a bloodthirsty warmonger."

———

A quick review of the two years since George W. Bush took office may offer some light on why we are where we are. He came into office with the possibility of a recession, plus all the unhappy odor of his investiture through an election that could best be described as legitimate/illegitimate. America had learned all over again that Republicans had fine skills for dirty legal fighting. They were able to call, after all, on a powerful gene stream. The Republicans who led the campaign to seize Florida in the year 2000 are descended from 125 years of lawyers and bankers with the cold nerve and fired-up greed to foreclose on many a widow's home or farm. Nor did these lawyers and bankers walk about suffused with guilt. They had the moral equivalent of Teflon on their souls. Church on Sunday, foreclose on Monday. Of course their descendants won in Florida. The Democrats still believed there were cherished rules to the game. They did not understand that rules no longer apply when the stakes are immense.

If Bush's legitimacy was in question then from the start, his performance as President was arousing scorn. When he spoke extempore, he sounded simple. When more articulate subordinates wrote his speeches, he had trouble fitting himself to the words.

Then September 11 altered everything. It was as if our TV sets had come alive. For years we had been watching maelstrom extravaganzas on the tube, and enjoying them. We were insulated. A hundredth part of ourselves could step into the box and live with the fear. Now, an invasion from the Beyond! An Appearance! Gods and demons were invading the United States, coming in right off the TV screen. This may account in part for the odd, unaccountable guilt so many felt after September 11. It was as if untold divine forces were erupting in fury.

And, of course, we were not in shape to feel free

of guilt about September 11. The manic money-grab excitement of the Nineties had never been altogether separated from our pervasive American guilt. We were happy to be prosperous, but we still felt guilty. We are a Christian nation. The *Judeo* in *Judeo-Christian* is a grace note. We are a Christian nation. The supposition of a great many good Christians in America is that you were not meant to be all that rich. God didn't necessarily want it. For certain, Jesus did not. You weren't supposed to pile up a mountain of moolah. You were obligated to spend your life in altruistic acts. That was still one half of the good Christian psyche. The other half, pure American, was, as always: Beat everybody. One can offer a cruel but conceivably accurate remark: To be a mainstream American is to live as an oxymoron. You are a good Christian, but you strain to remain dynamically competitive. Of course, Jesus and Evel Knievel don't consort too well in one psyche. Human rage and guilt do take on their uniquely American forms.

Even before September 11, many matters grew worse. America's spiritual architecture had been buttressed since World War II by our near-mythical institutions of security, of which the FBI and the Catholic Church were most prominent, equal in special if intangible stature to the Constitution and the Supreme Court.

Now, all that was taking its terrible whack. Old and new scandals of the FBI were brought into high focus by the Hanssen case, which broke in February 2001. An ultra-devout Catholic, Robert Hanssen had been a Soviet mole for fifteen years. No one in the FBI could believe it. He had seemed the purest of the pure anti-Communists. Then after September 11 came the pedophile lawsuits against the Catholic Church, and that opened a grieving abyss of a wound in many a good Catholic home. It certainly wounded the priesthood grievously. How could a young or middle-aged man wearing the collar walk down the street now without suffering from the averted eyes and false greetings of the parishioners he met along the way?

Then there was the stock market. It kept sinking. Slowly, steadily, unemployment rose. The CEO scandals of the corporations became more prominent.

America had been putting up with the ongoing expansion of the corporation into American life since the end of World War II. It had been the money cow to the United States. But it had also been a filthy cow that gave off foul gases of mendacity and manipulation by an extreme emphasis on advertising. Put less into the product but kowtow to its marketing. Marketing was a beast and a force that succeeded in taking America away from most of us. It succeeded in making the world an uglier place to live in since the Second World War. One has only to cite fifty-story high-rise architecture as inspired in form as a Kleenex box with balconies, shopping malls encircled by low-level condominiums, superhighways with their vistas into the void, and, beneath it all, the pall of plastic, ubiquitous plastic, there to numb an infant's tactile senses, plastic, front-runner in the competition to see which new substance could make the world more disagreeable. To the degree that we have distributed this crud all over the globe, we were already wielding a species of world hegemony. We were exporting the all-pervasive aesthetic emptiness of the most powerful American corporations. There were no new cathedrals being built for the poor—only sixteen-story urban-renewal housing projects that sat on the soul like jail.

Then came a more complete exposure of the economic chicanery and pollution of the corporations. Economic gluttony was thriving at the top. Criminal behavior was being revealed on the front page of every business section. Without September 11, George W. Bush would have been living in the nonstop malaise of uglier and uglier media. It could even be said that America was taking a series of hits that were not wholly out of proportion to what happened to the Germans after World War I, when inflation wiped out the fundamental German notion of self, which was that if you worked hard and saved your money, you ended up having a decent old age. It is likely that Hitler would never have come to power ten years later without that runaway inflation. By the same measure, September 11 had done something comparable to the American sense of security.

For that matter, conservatism was heading toward a divide. Old-line conservatives like Pat Buchanan believed that America should keep to itself and look to solve those of its problems that we were equipped to solve. Buchanan was the leader of what might be called old-value conservatives, who believe in family, country, faith, tradition, home, hard and honest labor, duty, allegiance, and a balanced budget. The ideas, notions, and predilections of George W. Bush had to be, for the most part, not compatible with Buchanan's conservatism.

Bush was different. The gap between his school of thought and that of old-value conservatives could yet produce a dichotomy on the right as clear-cut as the differences between communists and socialists after World War I. "Flag conservatives" like Bush paid lip service to some conservative values, but at bottom they didn't give a damn. If they still used some of the terms, it was in order to avoid narrowing their political base. They used the flag. They loved words like *evil*. One of Bush's worst faults in rhetoric (to dip into that cornucopia) was to use the word as if it were a button he could push to increase his power. When people have an IV tube put in them to feed a narcotic painkiller on demand, a few keep pressing that button. Bush uses *evil* as a narcotic for that part of the American public which feels most distressed. Of course, as he sees it, he is doing it because he believes America is good. He certainly does. He believes this country is the only hope of the world. He also fears that the country is rapidly growing more dissolute, and the only solution may be—fell, mighty, and near-holy words—the only solution may be to strive for world empire. Behind the whole push to go to war with Iraq is the desire to have a huge military presence in the Middle East as a stepping-stone to taking over the rest of the world.

That is not a small statement, but this much can be offered directly: At the root of flag conservatism is not madness but an undisclosed logic. If you accept its premises, it is logical. From a militant Christian point of view, America is close to rotten. The entertainment media are loose. Bare belly-buttons pop onto every TV screen, as open in their statement as wild animals' eyes. The kids are getting to the point where they can't read, but they sure can screw. One perk for the White House, therefore, should America become an international military machine huge enough to conquer all adversaries, is that American sexual freedom, all that gay, feminist, lesbian, transvestite hullabaloo, will be seen as too much of a luxury and will be put back into the closet again. Commitment, patriotism, and dedication will become all-pervasive national values again (with all the hypocrisy attendant). Once we become a twenty-first-century embodiment of the old Roman Empire, moral reform can stride right back into the picture. The military is, obviously, more puritanical than the entertainment media. Soldiers are, of course, crazier than any average man when in and out of combat, but the overhead command is a major everyday pressure on soldiers and could become a species of most powerful censor over civilian life.

To flag conservatives, war now looks to be the best possible solution. Jesus and Evel Knievel might be able to bond together, after all. Fight evil, fight it to the death! Use the word fifteen times in every speech.

There is just this kind of mad-eyed mystique to Americans: the idea that we Americans can do anything. Yes, say flag conservatives, we will be able to handle what comes. We have our know-how, our can-do. We will dominate the obstacles. Flag conservatives truly believe America is not only fit to run the world but that it must. Without a commitment to Empire, the country will go down the drain. This, I would opine, is the unstated, ever-denied subtext beneath the Iraqi project, and the flag conservatives may not even be wholly aware of the scope of it, not all of them. Not yet.

Besides, Bush could count on a few other reliable

sentiments that will buttress the notion. To begin with, a good part of American pride sits today on the tripod of big money, sports, and the Stars and Stripes. Something like a third of our major athletic stadiums and arenas are named after corporations—Gillette and FedEx are two of twenty examples. The Super Bowl could only commence this year after an American flag the size of a football field was removed from the turf. The U.S. Air Force gave the groin-throb of a big vee overhead. Probably half of America has an unspoken desire to go to war. It satisfies our mythology. America, goes our logic, is the only force for good that can rectify the bad. George W. Bush is shrewd enough to work that equation out all by himself. He may even sense better than anyone how a war with Iraq will satisfy our addiction to living with adventure on TV. If this is facetious, so be it—the country is becoming more loutish every year. So, yes, war is also mighty TV entertainment.

——

More directly (even if it is not at all direct), a war with Iraq will gratify our need to avenge September 11. It does not matter that Iraq is not the culprit. Bush needs only to ignore the evidence. Which he does with all the power of a man who has never been embarrassed by himself. Saddam, for all his crimes, did not have a hand in September 11, but President Bush is a philosopher. September 11 was evil, Saddam is evil, all evil is connected. Ergo, Iraq.

The President can also satisfy the more serious polemical needs of a great many neocons in his administration, who believe Islam will yet be Hitler Redux to Israel. Protection of Israel is okay to Bush, electorally speaking, but it is also obligatory, especially when he cannot count on giving orders to Sharon that will always be obeyed. Sharon, after all, has one firm hold on Bush. With the Mossad, Sharon has the finest intelligence service in the Middle East if not in the world. The CIA, renowned by now for its paucity of Arab spies in the Muslim world, cannot afford to do without Sharon's services.

These are all good reasons Bush can find to go to war. As for oil, allow Ralph Nader a few statistics:

The United States currently consumes 19.5 million barrels a day, or 26% of daily global oil consumption. . . . The U.S. [has to import] 9.8 million barrels a day, or more than half the oil we consume. . . .

The surest way for the U.S. to sustain its overwhelming dependence upon oil is to control the sixty-seven percent of the world's proven oil reserves that lie below the sands of the Persian Gulf. Iraq alone has proven reserves of 112.5 billion barrels, or 11% of the world's remaining supply. . . . Only Saudi Arabia has more.

I would add that once America occupies Iraq, it will also gain a choke hold on Saudi Arabia and the rest of the Middle East. One can also propose that we wish to go into Iraq for the water. To quote a piece by Stephen C. Pelletiere in *The New York Times* of January 31:

> There was much discussion over the construction of a so-called Peace Pipeline that would bring the waters of the Tigris and Euphrates south to the parched Gulf states and, by extension, Israel. No progress has been made on this, largely because of Iraqi intransigence. With Iraq in American hands, of course, all that could change.

So, yes, oil is a part of the motive, even if that can never be admitted. And water could prove a powerful tool to pacify a great many heated furies of the desert. The underlying motive, however, still remains George W. Bush's underlying dream: Empire!

"What word but 'empire' describes the awesome thing that America is becoming?" wrote Michael

Ignatieff on January 5 in *The New York Times Magazine:*

> It is the only nation that polices the world through five global military commands; maintains more than a million men and women at arms on four continents; deploys carrier battle groups on watch in every ocean; guarantees the survival of countries from Israel to South Korea; drives the wheels of global trade and commerce, and fills the hearts and minds of an entire planet with its dreams and desires.

From Timothy Garton Ash in *The New York Review of Books,* February 13:

> The United States is not just the world's only superpower; it is a hyperpower, whose military expenditures will soon equal that of the next fifteen most powerful states combined. The EU has not translated its comparable economic strength—fast approaching the US $10 trillion

economy—into comparable military power or diplomatic influence.

Perhaps the most thorough explanation of this as yet unadmitted campaign toward Empire comes from the columnist Jay Bookman of *The Atlanta Journal-Constitution*. Back on September 29, 2002, he wrote:

This war, should it come, is intended to mark the official emergence of the United States as a full-fledged global empire, seizing sole responsibility and authority as planetary policeman. It would be the culmination of a plan 10 years or more in the making, carried out by those who believe the United States must seize the opportunity for global domination, even if it means becoming the "American imperialists" that our enemies always claimed we were.

Back in 1992, a year after the final fall of the Soviet Union, there were many on the right in

America, early flag conservatives, who felt that an extraordinary opportunity was now present. America could now take over the world. The Defense Department drafted a document which, to quote Jay Bookman once more,

> envisioned the United States as a colossus astride the world, imposing its will and keeping world peace through military and economic power. When leaked in its final draft form, however, the proposal drew so much criticism that it was hastily withdrawn and repudiated by the first President Bush. . . .
>
> The defense secretary in 1992 was Richard Cheney; the document was drafted by [Paul] Wolfowitz, who at the time was defense undersecretary for policy.

Now, as we know, Wolfowitz is deputy defense secretary under Rumsfeld.

Afterward, from 1992 to 2000, this dream of world domination was not picked up by the Clinton administration, and that may help to account for the intense, even virulent hatred that so many on the right felt during those eight years. If it weren't for Clinton, America could be ruling the world.

Obviously, that document, "Project for the New American Century," projected prematurely in 1992, had now, after September 11, become the policy of the Bush administration. The flag conservatives were triumphant. They could seek to take over the world. Iraq could be the first step. Beyond, but very much on the historical horizon, were not only Iran, Syria, Pakistan, and North Korea but China.

Of course, not every last country had to be subjugated. Some needed only to be brought into one or another species of partnership. To speak of China as existing in a symbiotic relationship with us is too exceptional a remark, however, to make without some projection into the likely underpinning. It is not inconceivable that some of the brighter neocons do foresee some fearful possibilities in our technological development down the road. Iraq and the Middle East can hardly be the end. Greater nonmilitary specters and perils loom for the future. A late-January piece in *The Boston Globe* by Scott A. Bass sets it forth:

> Research and development at American universities relies heavily on foreign students in the crucial fields of science, technology, engineering, and mathematics (the STEM fields). . . .
>
> If . . . trends continue, we will have too few domestic students earning advanced graduate degrees in the STEM fields to support our economic, strategic, and technological needs. The flow of young American scientists and engineers has been reduced to a trickle, with many other industrialized countries having a far greater proportion of students going into these fields.
>
> While foreign students are attracted to STEM fields at U.S. research universities, our own domestic students are not. Many have not been sufficiently encouraged, and others may have found the academic rigors of the STEM fields too challenging.

Between 1986 and 1996, foreign students earning STEM field Ph.D.s increased at a rate nearly four times faster than domestic students. In 2000, 43 percent of physical science Ph.D.s went to non-U.S. citizens.

Flag conservatives may yet be hoping to send some such message as this to China: "Hear ye! You Chinese are obviously bright. We can tell. We know! Your Asian students were born for technology. People who have led submerged lives love technology. They don't get much pleasure anyway, so they like the notion of cybernetic power right at their fingertips. Technology is ideal for them. We can go along with that. You fellows can have your technology; may it be great! But, China, you had better understand: We still have the military power. Your best bet, therefore, is to become Greek slaves to us Romans. We will treat you well. You will be most important to us, eminently important. But don't look to rise above your future station in life. The best you can ever hope for, China, is to be our Greeks."

In the 1930s, you could be respected if you earned a living. In the Nineties, you had to demonstrate that you were a promising figure in the ranks of greed. It may be that Empire depends on an obscenely wealthy upper upper class who, given the inbuilt, never-ending threat to their wealth, is bound to feel no great allegiance in the pit of its heart for democracy. If this insight is true, then it can also be said that the disproportionate wealth which collected through the Nineties may have created an all but irresistible pressure at the top to move from democracy to Empire. That would safeguard those great and quickly acquired gains. Can it be that George W. Bush knows what he's doing for the future of Empire by awarding these huge tax credits to the rich?

Of course, terrorism and instability are the reverse face of Empire. If the Saudi rulers have been afraid of their mullahs for fear of their power to incite terrorists, what will the Muslim world be like once we, the Great Satan, are there to dominate the Middle East in person?

Since the administration can hardly be unaware of the dangers, the answer comes down to the unhappy likelihood that Bush and Company are ready to be hit by a major terrorist attack. As well as any number of smaller ones. Either way, it will strengthen his hand. America will gather about him again. We can hear his words in advance: "Good Americans died today. Innocent victims of evil had to shed their blood. But we will prevail. We are one with God." Given such language, every loss is a win.

Yet so long as terrorism continues, so will its subtext, and there lies the horror to its nth power. What made deterrence possible in the Cold War was not only that there was everything to lose for both sides, but there was also the built-in inability on either side to be certain it could count on any particular human being to flip the apocalyptic switch over to world domination. In that sense, no final plan could be counted on. How could either of the superpowers be certain that the up-to-now wholly reliable human selected to push the button would actually prove reliable enough to obliterate the other half of the world? A dark cloud might come over him at the last moment. He could fall to the ground before he could do the deed.

This human unreliability does not apply, however, to a terrorist. If he is ready to kill himself, he can also be ready to destroy the world. The wars we have known until this era, no matter how horrible, could offer at least the knowledge that they would come to an end. Terrorism, however, is not attracted to negotiation. Rather, it would insist on no termination short of victory. Since the terrorist cannot triumph, he cannot cease being a terrorist. They are a true enemy, far more basic, indeed, than Third World countries with nuclear capability that invariably appear on the scene prepared to live with deterrence and its in-built outcome—agreements after years or decades of passive confrontation and hard bargaining.

If much of what has been argued so far has been restricted to neocon mentality, there is a wing of the flag conservatives' campaign to invade Iraq that does have liberal support. Part of the liberal media, columnists at *The New Yorker* and *The Washington Post* and some at *The New York Times,* is joined with Senators Hillary Clinton and Dianne Feinstein, Joe Lieberman and John Kerry, in acceptance of the idea that perhaps we can bring democracy to Iraq by invasion. In a carefully measured appraisal of what the possibilities might be, Bill Keller speaks on *The New York Times* op-ed page on February 8 of a war that might go quickly and well:

> Let's imagine that the regime of Saddam Hussein begins to crumble under the first torrent of cruise missiles. The tank columns rumbling in from Kuwait are not beset by chemical warheads. There is no civilian carnage. [Even so] a victory in Iraq will not resolve the great questions of what we intend to be in the world. It will lay them open.
>
> [Is] our aim to promote secular democracy, or stability? Some, probably including some

in Mr. Bush's cabinet, will argue that it was all about disarmament. Once that is done, they will say, once Saddam's Republican Guard is purged, we can turn the country over to a contingent of Sunni generals and bring our troops home in 18 months.

Or perhaps, argues Keller, we will fashion a real democracy in Iraq after all, and the Middle East will benefit. It is as if these liberal voices have decided that Bush cannot be stopped and so he must be joined. To commit to a stand against fighting the war would guarantee the relative absence of Democrats at the administration tables that will work on the future of Iraq. It is an argument that can be sustained up to a point, but the point depends on many eventualities, the first of which is that the war is quick and not horrendous.

The old Bill Clinton version of overseas presumption is present. The argument that we succeeded in building democracy in Japan and Germany and therefore can build it anywhere does not necessarily hold. Japan and Germany were countries with a homogeneous population and a long existence as nations. They each were steeped in guilt at the depredations of their soldiers in other lands. They were near to totally destroyed but had the people and the skills to rebuild their cities. The Americans who worked to create their democracy were veterans of Roosevelt's New Deal and, mark of the period, were effective idealists.

Iraq, in contrast, was never a true nation. Put together by the British, it was a post–World War I patchwork of Sunnis, Shiites, Kurds, and Turkomans, who at best distrusted one another intensely. A situation analogous to Afghanistan's divisions among its warlords could be the more likely outcome. No one will certainly declare with authority that democracy can be built there, yet the arrogance persists. There does not seem much comprehension that, except for special circumstances, democracy is never there in us to create in another country by the force of our will. Real democracy comes out of many subtle individual human battles that are fought over decades and finally over centuries, battles that succeed in building traditions. The only defenses of democracy, finally, are the traditions of democracy. When you start ignoring those values, you are playing with a noble and delicate structure. There's nothing more beautiful than democracy. But you can't play with it. You can't assume we're going to go over to show them what a great system we have. This is monstrous arrogance.

———

Because democracy is noble, it is always endangered. Nobility, indeed, is always in danger. Democracy is perishable. I think the natural government for most people, given the uglier depths of human nature, is fascism. Fascism is more of a natural state than democracy. To assume blithely that we can export democracy into any country we choose can serve paradoxically to encourage more fascism at home and abroad. Democracy is a state of grace attained only by those countries that have a host of individuals not only ready to enjoy freedom but to undergo the heavy labor of maintaining it.

The need for powerful theory can fall into many an abyss of error. One could, for example, be wrong about the unspoken motives of the administration. Perhaps they are not interested in Empire so much as trying in good faith to save the world. We can be certain at least that Bush and his Bushites believe this. By the time they are in church each Sunday, they believe it so powerfully, tears come to their eyes. Of course, it is the actions of men and not their sentiments that make history. Our sentiments can be flooded with love within, but our actions can produce the opposite. Perversity is always looking to consort with the best motives in human nature.

David Frum, who was a speechwriter for Bush (he coined the phrase "axis of evil"), recounts in *The Right Man: The Surprise Presidency of George W. Bush* what happened at a meeting in the Oval Office last

September. The President, when talking to a group of reverends from the major denominations, told them,

> You know, I had a drinking problem. Right now, I should be in a bar in Texas, not the Oval Office. There is only one reason that I am in the Oval Office and not in a bar: I found faith. I found God. I am here because of the power of prayer.

That is a dangerous remark. As Kierkegaard was the first to suggest, we can never know where our prayers are likely to go nor from whom the answers will come. When we think we are nearest to God, we could be assisting the Devil.

"Our war with terror," says Bush, "begins with al Qaeda, but it does not end . . . until every terrorist group of global reach has been found, stopped, and defeated." But, asks Eric Alterman in *The Nation*, what if America ends up alienating the whole world in the process? "At some point, we may be the only ones left," Bush told his closest advisers, according to an administration member who leaked the story to Bob Woodward. "That's okay with me. We are America."

It must by now be obvious that if the combined pressures of Security Council vetoes and the growing sense of world outrage, plus a partial collaboration of Saddam with the inspectors, result in long-term containment rather than war, if Bush has to turn away from an active invasion of Iraq, he will do so with great frustration. For he will have to live again with all the old insolubles! Deep down, he may fear that he will not have any answer then for restoring America's morale. Can it be that the prospect of bringing these troops home again will prove so unpalatable that he has to go to war? And will.

Speaking to the Senate, Robert Byrd said,

Many of the pronouncements made by this administration are outrageous. There is no other word. Yet this chamber is hauntingly silent. On what is possibly the eve of horrific infliction of death and destruction on the population of the nation of Iraq—a population, I might add, of which over 50 percent is under age fifteen—this chamber is silent. On what is possibly only days before we send thousands of our own citizens to face unimagined horrors of chemical and biological warfare—this chamber is silent. On the eve of what could possibly be a vicious terrorist attack in retaliation for our attack on Iraq, it is business as usual in the United States Senate.

We are truly "sleepwalking through history." In my heart of hearts I pray that this great nation and its good and trusting citizens are not in for a rudest of awakenings.

... I truly must question the judgment of any President who can say that a massive unprovoked military attack on a nation which is over 50 percent children is "in the highest moral traditions of our country." This war is not necessary at this time. Pressure appears to be having a good result in Iraq. ... Our challenge is to now find a graceful way out of a box of our own making. Perhaps there is still a way if we allow more time.

If I were George W. Bush's karmic defense attorney, I would argue that his best chance to avoid conviction as a purveyor of false morality would be to pray for a hung jury in the afterworld.

For those of the rest of us who are not ready to depend on the power of prayer, we will do well to find the rampart we can defend over what may be dire years to come. Democracy, I would repeat, is the noblest form of government we have yet evolved, and we may as well begin to ask ourselves whether we are ready to suffer, even perish, for it rather than preparing ourselves to live in the lower existence of a monumental banana republic with a government always eager to cater to mega-corporations as they do their best to appropriate our thwarted dreams with their elephantiastical conceits.

Appendix

NOTES ON A LARGE
AND UNANCHORED UNEASINESS

A word would be appropriate here about the interview I did with *The American Conservative*, December 2, 2002, a magazine published by Pat Buchanan and Taki Theodoracopulos and edited by Scott McConnell. The piece was titled (by them) "Why I Am a Left Conservative." Much of what I said there was put into the address to the Commonwealth Club.

More remains, however, from that magazine and from the interview with Dotson Rader. Since I think it can serve the purpose of this book, I include such sections in this Appendix.

FLAG CONSERVATIVES

Back when the Soviet Union fell, flag conservatives felt this was their opportunity to take over the world. They felt they were the only people who knew how to run the world. So their lust was fierce. They were furious when Clinton got in. That was one reason he was so hated. He was frustrating the world takeover. That seemed so open, so possible to their point of view, back in 1992. How that contributed to their hatred of Clinton! This attitude, I think, deepened and festered through the eight years of Clinton's administration. Moreover, they loathed the ongoing increase in sexual liberties. White House principals may not talk to one another in private about this, but a key element in their present thought, I suspect, is that if America becomes an empire, then of necessity everything in America that needs to be *cleansed* will be affected positively. By their lights! If America grows into the modern equivalent of the Roman Empire, it will be necessary to rear whole generations who can serve the military in all parts of the world. It will put a new emphasis again upon education. Americans, who are famous for their inability to speak foreign languages, will suddenly be encouraged and over-encouraged to become linguists in order to handle the overseas tasks of empire. The seriousness of purpose will be back in American life. These are, I suspect, their arguments.

What they don't take into account is the exceptional perversity of human affairs. Indeed, the entire scheme could fail. The notion reeks of overweening hubris.

DREAD: A LARGE AND UNANCHORED UNEASINESS

This war, if it proliferates over the next decade, could prove worse in one respect than any conflict we have yet experienced. It is that we will never know just what we are fighting for. It is not enough to say we are against terrorism. Of course we are. In America, who is not? But terrorism compared to more conventional kinds of war is formless, and it is hard to feel righteous when in combat with a void, for then the action smacks of rage and relative impotence, a frightful combination that deprives warrior and citizen alike of any sense of virtue. Be it said, the sense of national virtue is crucial to waging a war.

———

We violate Christianity with every breath we take. Equally do the Muslims violate Islam. We are speaking of a war then between two essentially unbalanced and inauthentic theologies. It may yet prove to be an immense war. A vast conflict of powers is at the core, and the motives of both sides do not bear close examination. At bottom, the potential for ill is so great that we can wonder if we will get through this century. We could come apart—piece by piece, disaster after disaster, small and large, *long* before a final conflagration.

AMERICAN CONSERVATIVE: The conflict between communism and capitalism seems so much more sensible and manageable in comparison.

NORMAN MAILER: Looking back, it was kind of logical. Capitalism and communism had clear and opposed objectives, but neither was ready to destroy the world. Certainly, the more that conflict ebbed into its end days, the less danger was present that the big bang would come.

AMERICAN CONSERVATIVE: You have cast the fight as Allah versus moolah, Islam versus money. If ours is indeed a post-Christian society in which materialism is the highest good and it takes a faith to fight a faith, are they not better suited to combat us?

NORMAN MAILER: Are they better suited? No, I don't think so. It does seem to me, on the face of it, that if we did nothing in terms of attacking them, that might delay such a war for fifty years. The next argument would be, well, can we afford to delay? We can win it now and we might lose it in fifty years. But my notion is that this war is so unbalanced in so many ways, so much power on one side, so much true hatred on the other, so much technology for us, so much potential terrorism on the other, that the damages cannot be estimated. It is bad to enter a war that offers no clear avenue to conclusion. Terrorism can proliferate. It is not that complicated to be an effective terrorist, after all. Pick up the phone, make a call, and disrupt traffic for half a day. The real question is how pervasive can terrorism get, not whether you can wipe it out. There will always be someone left to act as a terrorist. If we try to become an empire, the real question will soon be whether we are able to live with terrorism at the level that the Israelis, let us say, are living with it now.

A NOTE ON PRESIDENTS

Given the rigors of presidential campaigns, most men who run successfully for president have been rubbed down by then to their lowest common denominator. *They are not all that impressive any longer as*

humans. So it is worth taking a quick look at their re-
sources and their foibles. Compulsive adoration of
our leaders is poison, after all.

I once sat on Reagan's left at a lunch for eight people.
This was in 1972, at the convention that nominated
Nixon for the second time. I spent the entire meal
trying to figure out a tough question to ask him. I always found that if you meet someone's eyes, a good
question can come to mind. But for two hours he sat
there at the head of the table, perfectly calm and
pleasant, and kept making jokes and talking. It was a
lightweight conversation. The physical impression
of him was that he had about as much human specific
density as, let's say, a sales manager for a medium-size
corporation in the Midwest. That kind of modest,
mild, well-knit heft was in his bearing. During those
two hours, he chatted with all six *Time* reporters at
the table, but his eyes never met mine, and I found
myself unable to come up with that tough question.
It became a matter of decorum. The mood was too

genial. It occurred to me that all through his political life, he probably, if he could help it, never spent time talking to anyone who was of no use to him. He was, be it said, an instinctive climber who scaled the face of success with great skill. That was his gift. Soon enough, he was surrounded by people who had many powerful (if self-serving) ideas and they knew how to illumine him to the point where they could wind him up. Then he could do his special stuff. At the time, he had an enormous impact on old-line conservatives, because they thought he was one of them. I suspect he had about as much to do with them as a screen star does with an agricultural laborer.

I would guess George W. Bush can tell when one of his experts knows what he's talking about and when he's only pretending he knows. So I would assume he makes his decisions in opposite fashion to his predecessor. Bill Clinton made a point of surrounding himself with people who might be 90 percent as intelligent as himself but never his equal, never more intelligent. Clinton, therefore, was always the brightest guy in his circle. Whereas Bush is smart enough to know that he couldn't possibly do the same or the country would be run by morons. In contrast, he looked to get bright people around him: Rumsfeld, Cheney, Rice, Powell. And when they start arguing, Bush has an ear for who is most incisive at a given moment. He can pick up a hint of the inauthentic in even a seasoned expert's voice. I'm speaking as a novelist now. Bush has a bullshit detector. Since different experts have days when they're better than on other days, Bush, on a given morning, decides that Expert A's voice sounds the best. Three days later, Expert D comes in better. The result is that he's always tweaking his policies just a little. If that is his one intellectual strength, he still has the persona of a fraternity president, sententious, full of cant, pleased with his assertions and always indifferent to their lack of verisimilitude and/or specificity. Mottos and platitudes are steak tartare to him. He knows exactly what he's doing. So, that one good half of

America, composed of religious people who are not particularly political, is with him all the way. Give us more of your mottos and platitudes, they ask. Spice them, please, with your incomparably holy touch of mendacity.

IMMIGRATION

AMERICAN CONSERVATIVE: Our side of the immigration debate generally feels that America is getting transformed into something less like the country we understand and are used to. It seems a kind of foreign place. It is not an argument we often use, but that is in the back of it. Have you thought much about the more multicultural America? What are its possibilities? What are its limitations?

NORMAN MAILER: Given the modern world of technology, I don't know whether the race or culture question is paramount. The long-term tendency for the world is to have no races. Technology has become the dominant culture in existence and may soon be the only real culture. The similarities between computer users all over the world may now be far greater than their differences in ethnicity.

AMERICAN CONSERVATIVE: Go back to the integrity of races. I know it is a politically incorrect thought, but it doesn't have to be expressed with rancor. It might be interesting.

NORMAN MAILER: Let me put it this way: I don't see immigration as a pressing problem other than that it gets some white people so furious that they can't think about more important things. They feel America is being lost. All right, America is being lost, but in ways that have nothing to do with races or excessive immigration. America, for one example, is being lost through television.

Because in advertising, mendacity and manipulation are raised to the level of internal values for the advertisers. Interruption is seen as a necessary concomitant to marketing. It used to be

that a seven- or eight-year-old could read con-
secutively for an hour or two. But they don't do
that much anymore. The habit has been lost.
Every seven to ten minutes, a child is interrupted
by a commercial on TV. Kids get used to the idea
that their interest is there to be broken into. In
consequence, they are no longer able to study as
well. Their powers of concentration have been re-
duced by systematic interruption. Add to that our
present-day classrooms. Does anybody ever say
that one reason our education is such a blighted
mess is that just about all schools now use fluorescent lights? Why? Because they cost less. I
would say that in the final count of dollars and
cents, they cost more, because the kids are less
productive. What characterizes fluorescent light
is that everybody looks 10 percent plainer than
they do under incandescent bulbs. Fluorescent
tubes offer a sickly light. Skin looks washed-out
and a bit livid. If everybody seems uglier than
they are normally, why then, everyone naturally
grows a little depressed. They begin to think,

What am I doing with all these plain-looking people? Aren't I worth more?

This little matter does contribute to the deterioration of the powers of concentration. Bad architecture, invasive marketing, ubiquitous plastic—such deleterious forces bother me much more than immigration. I could go on about this. Our first problem is not immigration but the American corporation. That is the force which has succeeded in taking America away from us.

IMPERIAL PLASTIC

NORMAN MAILER: Live in a technological environment long enough and you begin to feel as if your soul is frayed. A curious process has been going on in America for many years. You could term it the dumbing down of Americans, as if we have become cruder in certain ways as a reaction to a terribly uncomfortable time of coming to grips with technology, which is essentially antipathetic to the part of ourselves we love best—that creature who senses and can enjoy life. At this point in existence we're being asked to substitute power for pleasure.

Technology says to you, Fellow, get it through your head: You're going to have a little less pleasure from now on but much more power. That's technology's credo. And it opens a tendency for many of us to become narcissistic and power-driven. (And icy within.) Working in a technological environment, what do you have under your fingertips? Plastic. We all know plastic doesn't feel as good as wood, or skin. Even metal offers more to the touch, but the aim of technological society, ultimately, is to work everything over to plastic—woods, metals, flowers, food if they can do it, and indeed they've virtually accomplished that with the astronauts' nutrient packages.

Take commercial airplanes, for example. Getting on one is always a hellish experience. Not because you fear the plane is going to crash, but you are put into a totally plastic environment, you are hermetically sealed, you are engaged willy-nilly in the collective aura and psychic emissions of sixty, eighty strangers in a confined space. Even the air is fake. So it is a specifically unpleasant experience. And the airlines have been trying intermittently for the last fifty years to make the experience less unpleasant. The rest of the time they are looking to reduce amenities and squeeze out more money. Ah, the pangs of conscience, pro and con, within capitalism!

ISRAEL

These remarks on Israel are tentative. It cannot be otherwise. The pain of being a Jew is that one feels responsible for what all other Jews do. For to be Jewish is to live with the echo of a thousand years of alienation. To defend my own people proves as difficult for me then as it is to criticize them. I am not at ease with myself when I speak of Israel, or of Jews. All the same, some of what follows may be worth saying. I do not know that these thoughts are in all that many other places.

NORMAN MAILER: It is in the interest of the Arab nations to have Israel as the great villain. Although I'm Jewish, bone and blood, I'm not a patriotic Jew in the sense of Israel right or wrong, my Israel. I don't have those feelings. But I do think that the end of the Holocaust gave us one grand example of how inhuman the sheiks and leaders at the top of many an Arab nation were then. They could've said, "Let these Jews have that land. It's not going to hurt us. We might even be able to use each other to good purpose." They didn't. They chose to see these Holocaust survivors as the enemy. They used Israel to divert hatred away from their own regimes.

I expect high Saudi officials might well be content these days that the Israelis have an immense Palestinian problem. Because if they didn't, the Saudis might. The Palestinians, given their history, are probably less malleable to the dictates of Islamic extremism than other Arab peoples in the various Muslim establishments. Not all the Palestinians are even Islamic. They could prove a difficult mixture for countries like Saudi Arabia to deal with. So the Saudis now have a wonderful ploy: They use the Palestinians as their justification to hate Israel, when in fact they look upon Israel as their safeguard against the Palestinians.

AMERICAN CONSERVATIVE: Can we address more generally Israel and its unavoidable existential dilemma, which is the Palestinians?

NORMAN MAILER: Well, I start with a set of simple, unsophisticated notions about Israel. It was such a small country when it began. If the Arab leaders had had any kind of human goodness in them, they could have said, These people have been through hell. Let's treat them with Islamic courtesy, the way we are supposed to treat strangers. Instead, they declared them the enemy. The Israelis had no choice but to seek to become strong and ally themselves with us. In the course of doing so, some of the best aspects of Jewish nature—

irony, wit, the love of truth, the love of wisdom and justice—suffered internal depredations.

The prevailing attitude over the decades demanded that they become good farmers, good technicians, good soldiers. No need to use the minds for fine-tuning anymore. Do not even speak of hearts. "Be there. You're needed," became the overriding virtue.

Since it was a matter of saving their country, everything changed. *Quantity changes quality,* which may be the best three words Engels ever wrote. Quantity changes quality. As the Israelis became tougher, so they lost any hard-earned and elevated objectivity, any high and disinterested search for social value. The logo became Israel, my Israel. That was inevitable. It is also tragic, I think. Israel is now one more powerhouse in the world. But what they've lost is special. Now they treat the Palestinians as if they, the Israelis, are the Cossacks and the Palestinians are ghetto Jews. You know, the older you get, the more you begin to depend upon irony as the last human element you can rely on. Whatever exists will, sooner or later, turn itself inside out.

AMERICAN CONSERVATIVE: Do you think there is any way they can escape that dilemma with the Palestinians?

NORMAN MAILER: I don't see how. Not right now. It may be that what they feel is that if they don't gamble now, they will be destroyed later. If a war with Iraq ends with Americans installed there, Israel could feel more secure for decades to come. But it could prove a dangerous support. For a good many powerful Americans, the future question in Empire might become: How much is our support of Israel still to our advantage and how much to our disadvantage? The realpolitikers in the American establishment have to have mixed feelings even now about Israel. The neocons may feel this is their best shot, this is the moment when they have to take a chance because if they don't now, Israel is likely to be doomed ten, twenty, thirty years down the road.

But again, I say, You don't gamble that way.

I've always been thoroughly opposed to gambling with your last thousand bucks. Especially if you have a family. That is one reason I am a Left-Conservative. That is the conservative part of me.

AMERICAN CONSERVATIVE: What's your opinion of Ariel Sharon?

NORMAN MAILER: He is what he is. A brute. A power-house general. I think his defense would be: "I am what fate has made me." If he had lived in the ghetto, he would have been one of the stronger men there and probably one of the more disliked. But now he is an Israeli. What is obvious, what stands out in most Israelis, is that they are patriots. My God, they are. After Hitler, how could they not be? In that sense, I am sure Sharon thinks he is doing the only thing he can do, that he is doing the right thing. Just as I was going on earlier about Christians having this great unspoken guilt that they are not compassionate but greedy, so I think there is a similar inner crisis in Israel. I think they are ready to say: We are no longer humanists. We've become the opposite of ourselves. Still, we protect the country. We dare the un-known. If Saddam unloads on us? If a large part of Israel is lost to such a war? Well, sometimes one must undergo serious surgery. I think the Sharons are ready for that. Of course, the neo-cons here will not be losing their own arm or leg or lungs.

I would add that it is indeed a prodigious gamble for Israel. America could win easily over Iraq, but if Saddam has a Samson complex, what would his last act be? Might he hit Israel at the end with everything he's still got? At that point, he is a very dangerous man, since he has noth-ing more to lose. He would never dare to attack Israel first. That would certainly destroy him. He wouldn't even dare, I think, to allow terrorists to do it for him, because of the obvious reason that it would be too easy to trace it to him. But if Saddam has lost everything, then the likelihood is that he will pull down the columns of the tem-

ple: He will be ready to rest as history's super-
terrorist.

A NOTE PRECEDING THE END NOTE

The title of this publication was decided upon before we knew whether the United States would be at
war by the time this appeared in print or whether, for
that matter, the war might already be over.

I must say that the choice of title occasioned no
hesitation. War is a state of mind as well as a series of
martial events, and in that sense we have certainly
been at war with Iraq for many a month and probably will continue to be at war after the immediate
hostilities end.

The point I am trying to make is stated in the
title. Why? Why are *we* at war? Why are we living
with a state of mind that knows we are at war and
there is nothing we can do about it? Not now, not at
this juncture.

Enough. Since this all began with 9/11, let us
conclude with a thought or two on that.

END NOTE

Once, in the Democratic primary of 1969, I ran for
mayor of New York in the hope that a Left-Right
coalition could be formed and this Left-Right pin-
cers could make a dent in the entrenched power of
the center. The best to be said for our campaign was
that it had its charm. I am not so certain, however,
whether the basic idea must remain eternally without wings. It may yet take an alchemy of Left and
Right to confound the corporate center. Back then,
our notion was built on the premise that we did not
really know the elements of a good, viable society.
We all had our differing ideals and morals and political desires but rarely found a way to practice
them directly. So, we called for Power to the Neighborhoods. We suggested that New York City become
a state itself, the fifty-first. Its citizens would then
have the power to create a variety of new neighborhoods, new hamlets, villages, and townships, all built
on separate concepts, core neighborhoods founded
on one or another cherished notion of the Left or the

Right. One could have egalitarian towns and privileged places or, for those who did not wish to be bothered with living in so detailed (and demanding) a society, there would be the more familiar way, the old way of doing things—the State of the City of New York, a government for those who did not care, just like old times.

It was a menu for social exploration and experiment. If we had been elected, we might have ended with everything in an abysmal mess. It was a wicked scheme, since we had (just like our nation's current imperative to go to war with Iraq) no real notion of how it would all turn out, which is the essence of the wicked—up the ante and close your eyes while you wait for the turn of the card.

Nonetheless, some germ of the idea of a society open enough for people to live intense social lives still appeals to me. I repeat: We do not really know what works in a modern society, but the odds against flourishing in a society of the center (given its potentiality to narrow the exits and promote a single, central, secure point of view) may prove to be the least good answer of all. Until the Left and that part of the Right that is still loyal to its old values can come to recognize that no matter their essential differences, they also share one profound value they might look to protect in common—the vulnerable dignity of the human creation. At present, we are all obliged to travel willy-nilly into the vain land of corporate hegemony, with its self-serving notion that democracy is a nutrient to be injected into any country anywhere, a totally oppressive misconception of the delicate promise of democracy, which relies on the organic need to grow out of itself and learn from its own human errors.

By now, our nation has become a democracy that is bereft of a few of the essential elements. Nobody ever said, so far as I know, that a democracy should be a place where the richest people in the country earn a thousand times more than the poorest. Should the richest man in a town amass ten times more, even fifty times more, it is not hard to conceive of a reasonably decent society. When you get to the point where you're speaking of thousands to one, something outrageous is taking place. The people who feel this lack of balance probably make up two thirds of the country, but they don't want to think about it. They can't, after all, do a damn thing about it. We don't control our country. Corporate power is running this country now. The notion that we have an active democracy that controls our fate is not true. Was I ever able to vote on how high buildings could or should be? No. Was I ever able to say I don't want food frozen? No. Was I ever able to say I want tax money to pay for political campaigns, not interest groups? Nobody's ever been able to vote on many an item that truly matters in terms of how our lives are led. And, of course, we see the political process become more and more money-mechanized. We're on a power trip in which only one small fraction of America manages to participate.

They speak of pre-cancerous conditions in bodies, and I think we have a pre-totalitarian situation here now. I hope we'll muddle through, provided there are no more large disasters. There are pro-democratic forces in America that assert themselves when you don't expect them to.

But the situation is serious. If we have a depression or fall into desperate economic times, I don't know what's going to hold the country together. There's just too much anger here, too much ruptured vanity, too much shock, too much identity crisis. And, worst of all, too much patriotism. Patriotism in a country that's failing has a logical tendency to turn fascistic, just as too much sentimentality will corrupt compassion. Fascism in America is not going to come with a political party. Nor with black shirts or brown shirts. But there will be a curtailing of liberties. Homeland Security has put the machinery in place. The people who are running the country, in my opinion, simply do not have the character or wisdom to fight for the concept of freedom if we suffer horrors; no, not if we suffer dirty bombs, terrorist attacks on a huge scale, virulent diseases. The notion that you're going to have your freedom saved by people who work for security agencies is curious at best. They're on a one-way street. Anything bad of that sort is very bad for them. So they're going to do their utmost to restrict the freedom of people during critical situations. In the final analysis, democracy is inimical to security. Americans have to be willing to say at a certain point that we're ready to take some terrorist hits without panicking, that freedom is more important to us than security.

Let's suppose ten people are killed by a small bomb on a street corner in some city in America. The first thing to understand is that there are 285 million Americans. So, there's one chance in 28.5 million you're going to be one of those people. By such heartless means of calculation, the three thousand deaths in the Twin Towers came approximately to one mortality for every ninety thousand Americans. Your chances of dying if you drive a car are one in

seven thousand each year. We seem perfectly ready
to put up with automobile statistics.

DOTSON RADER: What is dangerous about what you
    are saying is that it implies there is a tolerable
    level of terror, and we have to accept it.

NORMAN MAILER: That's what I fear I am ready to
    say. There is a tolerable level to terror. Let's re-
    lieve ourselves of the idea that we have to remove
    all terror. Let's learn to live with the anxiety.

    What scared the hell out of me was a recent
    poll that indicated half the people in America are
    willing to accept a certain curtailment of their
    liberties in return for more security. If, already
    at this point, 50 percent of the people are ready
    to give up some of their liberties in return for
    that dubious security, then what's going to hap-
    pen if something truly bad ensues? Our belief
    that Americans are free individuals has suffered
    erosion in the last ten years from too much stock
    market and the greed it inspired. You know, Marx

and Jesus Christ do come together on one fundamental notion, which is that money leaches out all other values. Those ten years have done a lot of damage to the country's character. It's not as nice a place as it used to be.

I must say it again: In a country where values are collapsing, patriotism becomes the handmaiden to totalitarianism. The country becomes the religion. We are asked to live in a state of religious fervor: Love America! Love it because America has become a substitute for religion. But to love your country indiscriminately means that critical distinctions begin to go. And democracy depends upon these distinctions.

A good Englishman has a certain sense of the complexity of his national life. Even if he rides to hounds. The British have memory in a way we don't. That is the scariest single thing about American democracy to me: We don't have roots the way other countries do. Relatively, we are without deep traditions. So the transition from democracy to totalitarianism could happen quickly.

There could be fewer impediments here, those brakes and barriers that true conservatives usually count upon. But without the stops and locks, a nation can swing from one extreme to the other.

DOTSON RADER: Is there anything about this country that you love dearly?

NORMAN MAILER: Freedom. The freedom that I've had in my life. Who has ever had the opportunities I've had, the extraordinary freedom to be able to think the way I think, for better or worse? No, the best thing in America is that freedom. I had the great good luck that very few people have, to be a writer and earn a relatively independent income by the age of twenty-five. It didn't continue to be always that simple, but generally speaking, I've had more time to think than most people. I've had that advantage, that luxury. I can hardly hate the country. I don't want to make this a sentimental journey, but I have been treated very well.

You know, I once attacked J. Edgar Hoover on television in 1959, when he was still director of the FBI. I said he had done more damage to America than Joseph Stalin. Years later, under the Freedom of Information Act, I obtained my FBI file (which came to three hundred pages) and eighty pages of it were devoted to my remarks on that one TV show. Most of the FBI's comments were on the order of, Oh well, Mailer is just an arrogant fool. Yet the fact is that no matter how angry those people were, they didn't take me off in chains.

I have had great freedoms here in America, and I don't want to see them lost to the people who come after me. But I repeat: Freedom is as delicate as democracy. It has to be kept alive every day of our existence. So, yes, I do love this country. If our democracy is the noblest experiment in the history of civilization, it may also be the most singularly vulnerable one.

When you scratch an American he always says, "This is God's country." Well, I would suggest that the United States is God's most extreme and heartfelt experiment. So I lean toward thinking that the best explanation for 9/11 is that the Devil won a great battle that day. Yes—Satan as the pilot who guided those planes into that ungodly denouement.

DOTSON RADER: It's cinematic, isn't it?

NORMAN MAILER: Yes. As if part of the Devil's aesthetic acumen was to bring it off exactly as if we were watching the same action movie we had been looking at for years. That may be at the core of the immense impact 9/11 had on America. Our movies came off the screen and chased us down the canyons of the city. It makes sense to me that the Devil pulls off such a coup. I'm a great believer in Occam's razor: The simplest explanation that covers a set of facts is bound to be the correct explanation. If you can tell me why God wanted 9/11 to succeed, then I'll give way. But until then let me rely on the supposition that this was the Devil's big day.

ACKNOWLEDGMENTS

I want to thank David Ebershoff, Veronica Wind-
holz, and Judith McNally for their quick and incisive
contributions to this book.

28 Days

DATE DUE

MAR 1 6 2004		
APR 0 5 2004		
MAY 1 5 2004		
AUG 0 2 2004		
GAYLORD		PRINTED IN U.S.A.